PAINTING
AND DRAWING
WITH
LIQUID COLOURS

PAINTING
AND DRAWING
WITH
LIQUID COLOURS

Axel Brück

PAUL PETZOLD LIMITED
London

An Element technical publication
Produced by
Paul Petzold Limited, London, England
in association with
rotring Werke, Riepe KG, Hamburg, W. Germany

British Library Cataloguing in Publication Data
Brück, Axel
   Painting and drawing with liquid colours—2nd ed.
   1. Water-color painting—Technique
   I. Title
   751.42'2   ND2420

ISBN 0-946970-03-3

First published 1984
Second edition 1984

934 102

CONTENTS

1
INTRODUCING ARTISTCOLORS

Water-soluble colours

Today, the artist can choose what he needs from a wide variety of different water-soluble colours. All of these colours have special properties and, accordingly, find widely differing applications. Some types of colour medium have been designed for very specialised purposes, such as the retouching of photographs, while others, like watercolours or acrylics, serve as all-purpose artists' materials.

But anybody who has worked with these colours knows that they do have their shortcomings. For example, some water-soluble colours are more resistant than others to fading from the action of light. This is especially true of inks and watercolours (in both solid and liquid form). Whereas some colours are completely light-resistant, others seem to change or diminish almost as you watch.

Another problem for the artist is the transparency of the colours. If, for example, you wish to conceal a mistake in your work or would like to produce a very brilliant and heavily saturated hue, the colour needs to be opaque. Yet for some other purpose you might want to have this same shade as transparent as possible.

The ideal is a colour that stays soluble for long enough to lay a flat wash, but is also waterproof when dry. That would allow you to overpaint areas a second time without destroying the underlying colour. Additionally, a waterproof medium minimises the risk of damage to the finished artwork.

There are many other considerations to be taken into account when you are looking for the perfect colour medium and some of these are discussed later. For the purposes of this book I have chosen one painting medium in particular, which I will now describe.

rotring ArtistColor

rotring ArtistColor is a liquid watercolour which, in my opinion, comes as close as possible to the 'perfect' painting medium. I realise that a statement like this merits closer examination: for me, the perfect paint would be easy to use, universally applicable and would not fade through the action of light. Additionally, it should not be too expensive, but within easy reach of the hobbyist as well as the professional artist.

Take the most fundamental aspect – the mixing of different colours. This is (for different reasons) a problem for hobbyist and professional alike. As a beginner you may feel a bit unsure of how to achieve the desired hue, while if you are a professional your main priority may be fast and reliable repeatability. So, on the face of it, these factors seem to suggest that what is needed is a paint which is available, ready-mixed, in a wide variety of colours.

Apart from the fact that it is very expensive to keep on hand, say, 70 different bottles, pans or tubes of paint, this has some additional drawbacks. As a beginner, your first need is to acquire a 'feeling' for your colours and the confidence to recognise different hues and their relationships. You cannot do this by using pre-mixed paints. You really need to get involved with the paint of your choice — and this includes practising colour matching and mixing.

Colour mixing
Curiously enough, this is very difficult to do with paints that are available in a wide range of colours. Being spoiled for choice you cannot even start to find a systematic approach with them.

Quite understandably, almost all books on painting and drawing advise the reader to start with 'a small palette'; i.e. with as few colours as possible. The rotring ArtistColors are available in twelve different colours, including black and white. With the help of the mixing chart and dropper built into the cap of each bottle, you can mix any colour or tint required with a minimum of fuss and bother.

The professional artist may have different and quite specific needs. A graphic designer, for example, often has to use particular predefined tints for labels, company logos, trademarks and such like. According to Murphy's Law (which states that everything which *can* go wrong, will go wrong) even with 70 or so bottles ranged before him the artist *still* may not have exactly the right colour and will probably have to start mixing them anyway.

Here again, it is preferable to have a small number of basic colours that can be systematically mixed with the aid of a mixing chart. The dropper is very precise, so that it is only necessary to make a note of the number of drops of each colour used in order to be able to reproduce exactly the same shade again.

Other properties
Another feature of rotring ArtistColors is the fact that they will adhere to almost all imaginable surfaces, including those as widely differing as silk, or acetate cels or transparencies for overhead projectors. Thus, the same paint suits many different applications.

There is also great flexibility in choice of painting or drawing implements. While with brushes these ArtistColors handle just as well as ordinary watercolours, you can as easily apply them with an airbrush, a mouth diffuser, a roller or an isograph reservoir pen (down to .13mm in diameter!), or with SketchPens and lettering pens such as the rotring ArtPens. In fact, the possibilities are almost limitless and here I can give only an idea of what can be done.

Looking through the illustrations on the pages that follow, you will immediately see that the medium lends itself to all the 'classical' techniques of painting and drawing with watercolours as well as to exciting new techniques which open up a wide field for experimentation and innovation.

Apart from carrying on what you might call a 'full-time job' as paint, ArtistColors can be made to do more besides. Many people who paint in oils prepare underpainting with watercolour. Because they are consistently fade-resistant and also waterproof when dry, in most cases ArtistColors are more appropriate for this task. You can use them in combination with acrylic colours, gouaches and other types of medium.

The following chapters will tell you much more about these possibilities and how useful they might be to you. But for the absolute beginner, I also explore other subjects.

The rotring ArtistColors are not difficult to handle — on the contrary, they are what you might describe as very 'user friendly'. Nevertheless, some explanation of basic techniques is called for. If, for example, you have never previously laid a flat wash on a picture (i.e. covered a given portion with a completely even and ungradated layer of colour with no overlaps) you are bound to run into difficulties when attempting it for the first time. This applies, inescapably, to all transparent water-soluble colours.

On a simpler level, even the choice and care of your painting equipment, such as brushes, is of the greatest importance. All these problems will be discussed in the chapters that follow. Beginners as well as the more advanced reader should find many helpful tips and feel that this book provides a sound basis for further developments with this interesting medium.

Buying paint

When making your first purchase of materials (assuming you have decided to use water-soluble paints) you are immediately confronted with the difficulty of determining which colours to choose. Theoretically, it would be possible to buy five, or perhaps six different colours and then mix all the others from there. I believe, however, that the range of twelve rotring ArtistColors (including the black and the white) offer an optimal solution to this problem. A range of twelve colours is not so large that you are in danger of losing touch with the properties of your materials, yet it is not so small that colour mixing becomes tedious and/or difficult.

My advice, therefore, is to buy the whole set to start with and then to replenish it as you go along. Sooner or later you are bound to develop a marked preference for certain colours, while you may use others only occasionally. Nevertheless, it is quite practical to keep a complete set ready to hand so that you can take full advantage of the guidance offered by the mixing chart, which is designed to be used with the full set.

If you know exactly what you are doing you can, of course, use a smaller set, geared to your personal needs. In this context you might be wondering how long one of these bottles is likely to last you. It is unfortunately not possible to be absolutely precise about this because it depends so much on how you apply the colours. However, the contents of one bottle should be sufficient to cover several square feet at least.

The white is of special importance. It is not just used for colour mixing. A very small amount, added to any other colour, will make that colour opaque. Consequently, you have a choice between making the paint transparent or opaque at the final stage of application as well as at intermediate stages of mixing. If you adopt the classical watercolour painting technique, however, you have no need of white at all.

When it comes to the black, instead of the one in the ArtistColor range, you could use some other black indian ink. But I advise against this for general purposes, because, more often than not, the surface of another paint will look slightly different – either more shiny or more dull. Of course, you may actually want this effect. Usually, though, it will spoil the appearance of the finished work because variations in surface reflection make your pictures rather patchy.

To summarise: with a set of rotring ArtistColors, a good brush or two and almost any kind of working surface (for a beginner a good paper is recommended) you are ready to go. There are virtually no limits to what you can do – you are limited only by your imagination. The purpose of this book is to get you started.

2
PAINTING MATERIALS AND EQUIPMENT

Paints such as rotring ArtistColors are usually referred to as 'liquid watercolours' although, technically speaking, they are indian inks. However, such distinctions need not concern us here. The main point is that you can handle them exactly as if they were pre-thinned watercolours.

The brushes

These paints are usually applied with a brush to special watercolour paper. Brushes are available in a wide assortment of types and styles, ranging in price from a few pence to little short of £100. As a beginner, it can be quite difficult to choose the brush most suited to your purposes. One thing should never be forgotten – it is impossible to paint well with a bad brush. Although you do not need the best and most expensive sort when you are starting out, you should always try to buy the best you can afford.

The reasons for this are simple. Apart from the fact that a well cared-for red sable brush can last a lifetime, while a cheap one may need replacing after painting only one picture, the more expensive brushes tend to do their job much better. A good brush should have a 'fat' body of hair but a very fine tip so that it both holds plenty of paint and allows very delicate and detailed work. The hair should be very fine because this further increases its capacity to hold paint. Additionally, the hair must be resilient and 'springy'. After use, the brush should assume its original form.

Which brush?

When choosing a brush in the shop your preference should be for a good quality red sable (which is, alas, recognisable by its price). An all-purpose assortment of brushes for classical watercolour painting might consist of the following : a size 8–10 round brush, a size 4 round brush, and the same sizes in flat, chisel-edged brushes. Let me give you two tips: beginners tend to buy small brushes because they believe that they are the best for doing detailed work. This is not so. A good brush of the best quality can be very thick, yet always retain its fine tip so that you can use it for washes as well as detail. The second tip: when buying a brush, always test it by moistening its tip – a good artists' supplier will have a jar of water on his counter for this purpose.

If you have a limited budget, it is much better to buy only one brush of good quality than a number of mediocre ones. If you are buying just one, get a round one, size 6 – 8.

The paper

Although, in theory, you can use any type of paper that takes your fancy, it is advisable to start with standard watercolour paper mounted in blocks of 10 or 20 sheets. If you buy single sheets you have to mount them yourself which, although not difficult, takes some practice. This does not apply to the heaviest handmade papers which are thick and resilient enough to be used as they are.

Watercolour papers have a 'right' and a

'wrong' side. The right side is sized with a solution of animal glue and the surface usually has a better finish with fewer impurities.

The quality, surface texture and other properties of a watercolour paper influence the application of the colour (and, thus, the impact of your work) to a surprising extent. It is best for a beginner to start with a block of medium-textured watercolour paper and to refrain from experiments until the intricacies of watercolour painting are no longer a mystery. Once that is achieved, a rich and fascinating field lies ready to be explored.

Other supports

Watercolours in pans (cake form) and tubes should only be used on the supports for which they are intended, i.e. papers and boards. But once you have opted for rotring ArtistColors you can do much more.

You can apply them to smooth surfaces like glass, Perspex, acetate film and polished metal. The only preparation you need to do in such cases is to clean the surface very carefully with ox-gall or simply with a solution of household detergent. You should never touch the surface with your hands while painting.

You cannot overpaint an area which is not thoroughly dry. The first layer must be either still completely wet (in which event application of a second colour will result in a mixture of both) or absolutely dry. If it is only half-dry you will only succeed in removing some of the paint already applied. Fortunately, ArtistColors dry quickly, so that this kind of technique is perfectly practical.

If you want to produce really large-scale works (which does not necessarily mean great works!) you can, of course, use large sheets of paper. But with ArtistColors you are not confined to paper: you can just as easily paint on mounted canvas or silk. These materials can either be primed (treated with a ground preparation which is used for oil paint or acrylics) or used as they are. For fun, I once tried to do a drawing on a silk T-shirt using rotring isograph drawing pens — which worked quite well and gave pleasing results.

You can also apply the ArtistColors to wood (as it is, or prepared as if for laquering), plastic toys, photographic papers and films — in fact, almost every kind of material and surface you can think of. In some instances, especially with smooth surfaces, it might be advantageous to cover the dry artwork with varnish.

Varnish

Normally, it is not necessary to varnish work done with ArtistColors. In fact, a varnish might even change the surface appearance or alter the overall colour balance slightly. But if, for example, you have painted a wooden toy (ArtistColors are non-toxic) which, subsequently, will be in for some rough treatment, then to make it more robust you should protect the surface with varnish. The most suitable varnishes are the type designed for acrylic paints: those containing solvents other than water might cause damage.

There are some interesting experimental techniques making use of varnishes, which I will discuss later on.

Setting up

Apart from the paint, brushes and paper, you do not need much to begin working. A palette for mixing your colours (and storing them while you work) is, however, essential. These are made of porcelain or white plastic and can be brought separately, but the ArtistColor set contains a mixing tray suitable for starting off. Furthermore, you need to clean your brushes frequently, so you should either have access to a tap or keep a few large jars of water standing by. It is best to have three, one for the warm colours (yellow, red), another for the cold colours (green, blue) and a third for a second rinse. In order to avoid contaminating the colours that you have carefully prepared, change the water frequently.

From time to time you will need to tilt the painting surface, for example, when applying a wash. The standard type of drawing board will allow you to do this, of course, but a block of wood or a thick book will do just as well.

Some people insist on using distilled water to thin their colours — not only rotring ArtistColors but all other makes of water-soluble colour. The reason given is that ordinary tap water may cause chemical reactions in the paint. Unfortunately, there is some truth in this; what is supposed to be drinking water is sometimes not even good enough to paint with. However, if you do not intend to keep your mixed and thinned paints for any length of time, it should be pefectly safe to use ordinary tap water.

Inevitably, in the course of working you will occasionally spill some of your precious colour where it is not wanted. So always keep a rag for mopping up. As long as ArtistColor remains wet, it can be washed out with water. Once it is dry, however, it is waterproof. If you want to remove it at that stage you need rotring cleaning fluid (that is used for black drawing ink).

Caring for your materials

Keep everything meticulously clean. A fingerprint on your paper may be completely invisible until it produces ugly patches or blotches in flat wash. Treat your brushes with respect. If you have followed my previous advice, they will be quite an expensive part of your equipment. Never leave them pointing downwards in the water jar because this is sure to ruin the tip. Immediately after use,

clean them under running water or in a large jar, reshape the brush by pulling it gently over the palm of your hand and place it upright in a jar or vase for drying. To avoid accidental drying, always keep a folded paper handkerchief handy, thoroughly soaked with water. When having to interrupt work suddenly, for example, to answer the phone, it is easy to lay the uncleaned brush down, gently folding the wet handkerchief around the tip.

If you keep your brushes in a tin or box, they must be absolutely dry before you put them away. You must also make sure that the tips are not squashed and cannot be damaged in any other way. The ArtistColors themselves do not need any special care apart from one point. It is best not to leave the bottles open for a very long time because the paint might evaporate. If this *has* happened you can re-thin it. It is best to use distilled water for this (see above).

Such precautions are basically common sense; you are not very likely to encounter any particular problems when working with rotring ArtistColors.

3
TOOLS
AND
TECHNIQUES

The 'normal' way (if there is any such thing as a normal way in art!) to use watercolours is with a brush, on paper. But in my opinion the best and, incidentally, the quickest way to become really well-acquainted with what a paint can do and to discover the effects you can achieve, is to play around with it. Before you start wielding your brush it might be a rewarding exercise to try some other ways of applying colour to paper. This might also yield very interesting pictures.

Splattering

An old toothbrush or any other brush with stiff bristles can be used to 'splatter' paint on to the paper in the following way.

Place a few drops of ArtistColor in a wide section of your palette or a saucer and dip the toothbrush into the colour. The brush should be wet but not dripping. Now hold it — bristles up — at an angle over the paper, and draw a knife, a piece of stiff cardboard or the back of a comb firmly and with a relatively quick stroke over the bristles. You should practise this first on a sheet of newspaper in order to get it right. But once you have got the hang of it you can use this technique for parts of a picture or to build up an entire picture. The first technical illustration (ill. 3, p. 22) was done entirely in this way. The various shapes were cut out of ordinary paper. These 'masks' were then placed over the watercolour paper and weighted down so that certain areas were protected from the paint. In this way it is possible to achieve pictures of considerable complexity — though you need to have the patience to cut a new mask for each new shape to be introduced.

This technique is extremely simple and yields good results as long as you watch for two things. Do not 'splatter' too much paint on at a time. It can accumulate at the borders of the masks, creep under them and thus smudge the edges of the shapes. Secondly — and this is obvious — you should wait for the freshly applied colour to dry thoroughly before placing the next mask over your picture. But, as already mentioned, ArtistColor dries very quickly, so your patience should not be overtaxed.

Mouth-diffuser

Very similar, but much finer and more detailed effects can be achieved with the aid of a mouth-diffuser (or mouth-spray). This is a very simple and inexpensive instrument which is normally used to apply varnishes to finished paintings. A mouth-diffuser consists of two tubes positioned at right angles to each other. You insert one tube into the paint and blow through the other, thus generating a relatively fine spray. The method of application resembles that described for the stiff brush, but it is much more difficult, and you will need to practise regulating your breathing properly.

The technical principle is similar to that of the airbrush. Indeed, it would be better to use an airbrush if one were available, but as they are relatively expensive, a mouth-diffuser will do for the occasional use.

Illustration 4 (p. 22) was produced with a mouth-diffuser. It required quite a lot of breath and patience. The colours have been arranged in the sequence of the colour circle.

Airbrush

It is impossible to explain the use of an airbrush in just a few sentences, but it deserves to be at least mentioned here because it is so well-suited to rotring ArtistColors.

Unfortunately, good airbrushes are relatively expensive, though no more so than a top-quality red sable brush. It is probably the only instrument with which you can produce absolutely accurate flat and gradated washes with all types of water-soluble colours, including ArtistColors. If you have an interest in this kind of work, you should investigate air-brushes and the appropriate literature.

A number of the illustrations shown here have been produced with an airbrush. I will refer later to the techniques employed.

The technical drawing pen

A good technical drawing pen is the rotring isograph, with tubular nib and reservoir. They are commonly used for technical and architectural drawing. So far, their use for the artist has been limited by the fact that they have had to be filled with special drawing inks of not very appealing colours.

This situation has now completely changed because the whole range of rotring ArtistColors can be used with them. This even includes the white, which is normally a very problematical colour, due to the heavier and coarser pigment it contains.

The isograph easily lends itself to the techniques of coloured drawing, but it can also be used to correct mistakes or blemishes in pictures produced by other techniques. It can be filled with exactly the same colour as that mixed for the original work. Illustration 2 (p.19) consists entirely of very small dots of different colours, produced with a 0.13mm isograph.

Line drawings or mixtures of lines and dots are both possible using this method. You should, however, note the differences between artwork done with technical drawing pens and that produced with steel nibs (or rotring ArtPens). As a technical precision tool the isograph yields dots and lines of unvarying thickness. This gives an effect which differs substantially from that obtained with steel nibs or rotring ArtPens. (See below.) With these, the thickness of the lines can be varied considerably, depending on the pressure exerted on the nib. So dots, too, are bound to be fairly irregular.

This does not mean that one of these techniques is inevitably going to be better than the other. If you compare Illustration 2 (p. 19) with Illustration 7 (p. 27), which was done with rotring SketchPens, you will see that it is simply a question of the desired effect. Pictures done with isographs tend to look 'cool', they are usually more quiet, sedate or even introverted, while those done with steel nibs or SketchPens are more lively, spontaneous or extroverted. This remark, however, should not be taken as an absolute rule. I simply want to draw attention to the fact that there are generally marked and consistent differences in effects that are directly attributable to the painting or drawing instrument used. If you want to convey a certain feeling or mood in a picture, it is always helpful to find out which instrument and method will tend to stress these properties.

Sketch ArtPens and steel nibs

SketchPens have fine nibs (EF and F) which, as the name implies, are admirably suited to sketching. They can be used with converters of the type to be found in many fountain pens, so that you can fill them with any of the rotring ArtistColors and mixtures thereof. The same applies, incidentally, to the special pens produced for calligraphy and lettering, i.e. ArtPens. So the whole range of ArtistColors may be used with these two. Apart from the toothbrush and mouth-diffuser mentioned above, these are the more or less 'classical' instruments with which you can put colour on to paper. Their use is self-evident and easy although, of course, as with any technique, practice makes perfect. The easiest of all to handle are undoubtedly the rotring SketchPens. With these, the technical side of coloured drawing requires no practice at all, so they are well worth considering when starting out. Steel nibs produce the same type of line and dot as the rotring SketchPen but are much more difficult to handle.

Naturally, these remarks have nothing to do with the purely artistic aspect of creating a picture. However, if you have provided yourself with the most suitable means, this should allow you to concentrate on the artistic side without at the same time having to tackle technical problems.

If, on the other hand, you are seeking the special characteristics created by a brush, airbrush or whatever, I would advise you to first become acquainted with their technical idiosyncrasies by experiment and practice, before tackling 'serious' work. (For watercolour techniques see Chapter 5.)

Cleaning and maintenance

But before we go any further, I should add a few words on the cleaning and maintenance of the various instruments mentioned in this chapter. Although rotring ArtistColor is easy to use, a few basic and commonsense precautions should be taken.

Always replace the cap on ArtPens, SketchPens or isographs when not in use – even for a relatively short space of time. You should never leave these instruments lying around in direct sunlight, or any hot environment (even the glove compartment of a car) because they may dry out or leak. If this has happened, however, you will have to clean them out with rotring cleaning fluid. A good rinse with plain water does no harm when changing colours or – if you don't change colours – every few months or so.

If you observe these simple precautions, your drawing instruments should remain trouble-free and serviceable for a long time.

4
EXPERIMENTS
AND
EFFECTS

In the previous chapter I have described a technique for applying colour which I loosely term 'splattering'. This chapter describes some related processes.

Blowing

Many children are familiar with the following technique, which can lead to very intriguing results. You simply drop a little paint on to a sheet of paper (1 to 3 drops is enough — dark colours usually look best) and blow at it with the help of a drinking straw.

Holding the straw vertically over the paint while blowing will generate spidery, fanned-out forms, while holding it at an angle and moving it slightly from side to side while blowing will create shapes that are reminiscent of twisted treetrunks. Illustration 6 (p. 26) is an example.

Although this technique alone will not take you very far, it may be interesting to develop the basic forms into pictures. For example, you could add drawn or painted fantasy figures or landscapes to them. I have noticed that, apart from being fun, an approach like this often helps people to 'loosen up' and develop their imagination.

Drops

The next suggestion is a development of the basic technique of dropping paint on to paper. It is first necessary to make the paper completely wet. To do this, remove a sheet from your block, and let it soak for 2 to 5 minutes in cold water. Then take it out and wait for the superfluous water to drip off. Next, lay the paper flat on a piece of wood or some similar support and pin it down at the edges (in order to prevent an excess of warping and buckling when the paper starts to dry).

After these preliminaries comes the difficult part. You will have to wait a few minutes until the paper *just* starts to dry. If you wait too long, there will be no noticeable effect at all; if you start too early, the result will be a shapeless mess of colour.

At the right moment, which you will have to find by experiment, you simply drop a little colour on to the paper. (The height from which you let the colour fall also influences the effect.) The colour immediately starts to 'creep' over the paper, generating a result similar to the one shown in Illustration 11 (p. 36).

But watch out! The picture can continue to change for almost as long as the paper is wet. Because at first the effect may look too weak, the most common mistake is to use too much colour.

You should use only good quality watercolour paper for this technique; otherwise you will never be able to flatten it out properly when you have finished working.

Because the rotring ArtistColors dry waterproof, you can do something with them which is impossible with watercolours. After the picture has dried, you can start the whole process again. By repeating this cycle a number of times it is possible to build up some very interesting structures.

Taken at its face value perhaps this process amounts to no more than a passing amusement. But it has two particular advantages. On the one hand it tells you something about the interplay of your colours, which you might need to know when trying 'real' watercolour techniques. On the other, it can be used to generate fascinating backgrounds on which to build up paintings and drawings.

Structures

The next technique is actually a printing process, although you can use it to create only a single 'print'. The principle could hardly be simpler. You spread paint over a surface, place a sheet of paper over it and rub it, applying more, or less, pressure in different areas to influence the transfer of colour on to the paper.

Depending on the type of surface used, the consistency of the paint and the pressure applied, the effects you can produce in this way can vary enormously. Illustration 15 (p. 44) shows two examples of what can be achieved.

Rather than giving a long theoretical exposition I will simply explain how these two samples were done. Variations can be left to your ingenuity.

Example A. A sheet of heavy watercolour paper was thoroughly soaked in water and pinned to a board as described above. Some

ArtistColor was thinned considerably with water (about 20 to 30 parts of water to 1 part of colour). With a very broad brush this mixture was literally slopped over the paper, leaving a pool of wet paint. The next step was to crumple a sheet of tracing paper (slightly larger than the watercolour paper) into a tight ball and unfold it again without tearing. This was placed over the pool of paint and gently tapped until reasonably flat. It was then left untouched until the paint was almost completely dry. The two sheets were finally separated. This may take the better part of a day, so be patient – removing the tracing paper prematurely will ruin your effort.

Example B. In order to achieve this type of structure the colour should be very thick. Here some acrylic binder was added to the ArtistColor to turn it into a smooth paste which was then rolled on to a sheet of glass (with a roller normally used for inking lino cuts). A sheet of watercolour paper was placed on top of this and rubbed firmly. The paper was then removed. The structure remaining is influenced by the way in which you remove the paper – a quick, firm movement works best.

These few remarks should serve as a simple introduction to handling rotring ArtistColor. I will return to the subject of experimental techniques later on.

Page 18 1. This drawing has been executed entirely with isograph pens and undiluted ArtistColors. Variations in the intensity of colour have been achieved by varying the concentration of the dots.
Jutta Fischer-Brück

Page 19 2. In contrast to the first illustration this dragon was done with a nib (SketchPen EF and F). Note the differences in line thickness – the line is thicker or thinner depending on the pressure exerted.
Jutta Fischer-Brück

5
WATERCOLOUR TECHNIQUES

Although the 'classic' watercolour technique is really quite simple, it has some finer points which tend to elude the beginner.

If you have tried some of the experiments described in the previous chapters, you will already be familiar with the handling of your materials. We can now move on to something slightly more difficult.

Basic technique

The most important thing to remember when doing watercolour work is that you are dealing with transparent colours. You should therefore avoid both white and solid black. The lightest tone in your picture should be the white of the paper itself. Colours are lightened by thinning them with water, *not* by adding white. Conversely, very deep shadows or dark tones are produced by adding very small amounts of black or blue to another colour. The overall effect of a watercolour done in the classic style should be one of lightness, in every respect, and luminosity.

To achieve this it is usually best to start with the lightest tones and give your picture initial overall working with them. The results should be a very weak and hazy version of what you actually want to do.

The next step is to add slightly stronger (i.e. less diluted) tones, and you then repeat this procedure until you have achieved the desired depth. There is no risk of destroying the previously applied coat when working in this way, because rotring ArtistColors dry waterproof.

The one point to remember is that different colours tend to run or merge into each other when still wet. To avoid this, either wait until each painted area has dried before coating adjacent areas or leave a small white border between them.

Flat wash

A flat or gradated wash is the basis of practically all watercolour work, yet many people seem to find it very difficult to do. Any area that cannot be covered with a single brushstroke needs a wash, to avoid the tell-tale marks of individual brushstrokes.

To begin with, let us assume that you want to create a background covering the whole sheet evenly and without lines. Tilt the drawing board or support slightly (usually 15° to 30°) and dampen the paper with water. It should be evenly wet, without puddles or dry patches, which will show as ugly marks later on. Apply the water with a sponge. The easiest way is to use more water than is actually needed and then wait until the paper has soaked it up.

You should have the desired colour already mixed and a thick brush at hand, because good timing now is essential. Load the brush with plenty of paint (it should be almost dripping) and draw a stroke along the top of the paper. Re-load the brush and draw a second stroke below the first. Continue until you have filled the whole paper. You must apply each brushstroke before the preceding one starts to dry and also be sure to finish the whole job before the paper itself starts to dry.

Superfluous paint will run down the tilted paper and collect at the bottom, where it can be carefully removed with a dry brush, sponge or rag.

The same technique can be used to cover parts of your paper with a wash. Though in one way this is simpler because the plane to be covered is smaller, it is in fact more difficult because the borderline of the area to be covered with a wash can be quite complicated.

If, for example, you have a skyline with roofs, chimneys, etc. and want to add a blue sky you should turn the paper round so that you start at the complicated edge of the skyline and finish at what is now the bottom edge of the paper. You must always start a wash at the top and angle the support slightly, so that superfluous paint runs down. All this sounds more difficult than it really is and after a little practice you can try your luck with gradated washes.

Gradated wash

A gradated wash is basically very similar to a flat wash, the difference being that it either starts with a very faint colour which gradually becomes darker, or it starts with one colour which slowly turns into another.

Whether you want the darker part at the top or the bottom of your final picture, you must always apply the wash with the lighter tone at the top. If you do it the other way round, the excess of the darker colour runs down the paper so that you end up with a more or less even tone!

For a gradation from a light version of a colour to a darker, or vice-versa, you need to pre-mix the different tones, so that you can switch quickly from one to the next as you go along. Three different tones will probably be sufficient for a normal gradation. However, if you want a very great difference between the lightest and the darkest tone, you will need to prepare more.

The process is the same for a gradation from one colour to another. You must prepare in advance the two basic colours and some intermediate mixtures of them. Again, you turn the paper round so that you can start at the top. What makes this a bit more difficult is the fact that you have to judge the amount of paint you put onto the paper fairly accurately because an excess of paint or mixture running down the paper will obviously destroy the effect.

These techniques are the basis of all watercolour work. It is worthwhile practising them a few times before you actually use them in a painting.

Page 22 3. (top) Colour can be 'splattered' on to the ground using an old toothbrush. The resultant very irregular spots can create an interesting surface. Cut masks are used to prevent splattering beyond the defined areas.

Page 22 4. (bottom) The mouth diffuser is what you might call a poor man's airbrush. To do this kind of work requires some practice and an enormous amount of breath. This example, which represents a colour circle, took three days of near slavery to produce.

Page 23 5. The almost opalescent quality of this example has been achieved by optical mixing (using small amounts of unmixed colour which blend optically into different shades when seen from a normal viewing distance). A final coat of white enhances the effect.

Axel Brück

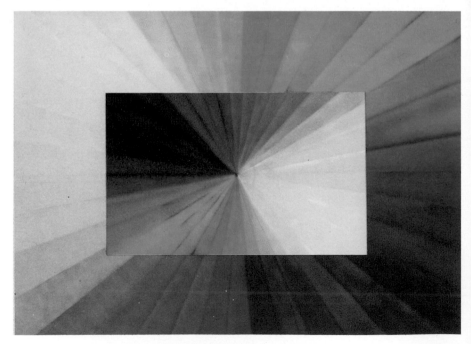

6
'DRY' AND 'WET' WATERCOLOUR

In older books on painting and drawing you sometimes find a distinction drawn between 'dry' and 'wet' watercolour. Although this terminology seems to have passed entirely out of use today, it distinguishes very neatly the two basic approaches to watercolour painting: with the dry watercolour technique, the paint is applied to dry paper; in the wet technique, to wet paper.

Dry watercolour
This is, essentially, what I have described as the 'basic' technique in the previous chapter. If you now compare this with what I have said about washes (which belong in the realm of wet watercolour painting), you can easily see that these techniques will lead to very different looking pictures.

Dry watercolour can be very precise and detailed. On dry paper, each individual brushstroke remains visible; colours do not merge or dissolve into each other. You can work slowly and methodically with this technique. Moreover, it is not only possible, but quite common practice to place various layers of colour on top of one another. This has the advantage of allowing you to correct mistakes made in previous layers. However, this method of correcting should· not be overused and, above all, you should never yield to the temptation to overpaint a mistake with white. This will be very obvious in the finished work as a badly concealed mistake.

Dry watercolour is a very interesting technique and it is quite wrong to look upon it as just a beginner's approach to watercolour painting. (Many people seem to think of the wet technique as the artist's 'crowning achievement'.)

Combined technique
One does not often see work that has been executed exclusively with the dry technique. More often than not it is combined with washes for skies, backgrounds or large uniform areas. Logically, indeed, this is the next step to take.

With traditional watercolours, because the paint remains water-soluble indefinitely, you have to work out quite carefully the best sequence in which to apply the washes and the 'dry' brushwork.

This problem does not arise with rotring ArtistColors, which dry waterproof. You can even paint a picture using the dry technique and then soak it and apply a flat or gradated wash. There is no risk of spoiling the work you have done previously. If you wish to apply washes between stages of 'dry' work, it is essential to be patient and wait until the paper is thoroughly dry. If the surface is at all damp, part of the brushwork may appear 'fuzzy' owing to some marginal 'bleeding'.

Illustration 8 (p. 30) has been executed entirely with dry watercolour techniques. The different effects of the colours have been achieved by diluting them by varying degrees. Compare this with the next picture (Ill. 9, p. 31)! Here the artist first worked over the whole picture using the wet technique (mostly with flat washes) and then (when the paint had dried, of course) added details and shadings with the dry technique.

The wet technique

I mentioned earlier that some people consider the wet watercolour technique superior to any other. This is not because this approach yields artistically superior results, but because it is the most difficult to do properly.

A well-executed wet watercolour is done in one stage; you paint directly on to the wet paper and you do not apply more paint to an area that has already been painted This makes corrections or changes impossible. Furthermore, you have to finish your painting before the paper dries, which always seems too soon! Re-wetting the paper is frowned upon by the purist because it is descernible in the finished work, at least, by the experienced eye.

The effect of a work entirely executed with the wet technique is fresh and spontaneous, and has enormous charm. But in order to do it properly, you really need to have mastered the finer points of drawing and painting to perfection. I often think that artists tend to make use of this technique simply to show off.

So, while I believe that you should try this technique if you are interested, I also think that you should be careful not to overestimate it — it is no better or worse in itself than the other techniques described here. The right choice simply depends on what you want to say or suggest with your work.

Conclusion

When you first become involved with painting or drawing, you will probably find yourself having to confront several different problems simultaneously. You might, for example, want to put effort into rendering subjects in a realistic style and at the same time wish to learn one of the techniques described here. In my view it is better to tackle these individual aspects separately. If you are not yet satisfied with the quality of your realistic rendering of subjects, *do not* attempt to perfect it at the same time as trying to teach yourself to lay flat or gradated washes. As long as you have difficulties with both aspects, you will never find out what went wrong! Experiment first with the paint and the various techniques described. Then, if you feel sufficiently confident, you are probably ready to tackle more 'serious' undertakings.

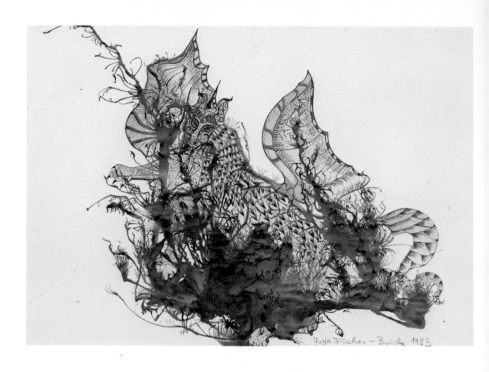

Jutta Fischer-Brück 1983

Above 6. Put a few drops of colour on a support and blow them apart with a drinking straw. The result may inspire you to devise some fantasy subject or to create a landscape that could never exist. The dragon was added as an isograph drawing.
Jutta Fischer-Brück

Right 7. The 'nightscape' of this painting owes part of its effect to the background, which was executed first in an absolute black and then covered with a transparent coat of blue. The bluishness derives solely from the application of the cloudy white final layer. *Axel Brück*

a.bück

-6-83

7
MIXED MEDIA I

So far, for the most part, we have been concerned with the more or less classical methods of watercolour work. But with rotring ArtistColors the range of applications and techniques is much wider. The following paragraphs give an idea of what else can be done.

ArtistColor and colour pencils
There are two types of colour pencil: those which are water-soluble (and give some semblance of watercolour technique when used on their own) and those which are waterproof. The latter variety can be profitably used in conjunction with ArtistColors. It is, for instance, quite possible to lay flat or gradated washes and then re-work them or simply draw over them with colour pencils. The effect is rather difficult to describe, but it rests mainly on the more 'liquid' feel conveyed by the ArtistColors as opposed to the 'powdery' effect of the colour pencils.

As both media are waterproof you can just as easily start with pencil work and then lay washes of ArtistColors on top. You can even put several layers on top of each other.

An interesting variation on this technique is to select a fairly rough paper and apply the liquid ArtistColor with a soft brush to cover the whole surface. You then work on it with a colour pencil which will catch only the raised parts of the paper surface. The result you get depends on selecting a paper of suitable structure and also on the pressure you exert on the pencil.

Gouache and ArtistColors
Gouache is an entirely opaque water-soluble paint. So-called poster colours or designer's colours are usually gouaches of inferior quality.

Although we will see later that it is perfectly possible to turn ArtistColors opaque by adding white, this is not very practical if you want to produce large opaque surfaces — for instance, when painting posters. In such cases it is simpler to apply the basic layer of colour in the form of a cheap gouache and then do the fine work of gradating and tinting with ArtistColors. Designers' colours, however, usually lack permanence, and you may also find that the range available is either too 'chalky' or too garish. The latter problem can be remedied by overlaying washes of ArtistColor, and permanence is probably your last concern when doing posters and related work.

The only major drawback with this technique is that gouaches do not dry waterproof. The best way out of this is to apply your ArtistColor with an airbrush. Alternatively, you can wait a few hours for the gouaches to dry thoroughly and then work with just one brushstroke at a time. This way, you are unlikely to damage the surface.

Acrylic paint and ArtistColors
Another rather interesting variation is to combine acrylic paint with rotring ArtistColors. This combination is much simpler to work with because acrylics dry entirely waterproof. You will probably find it easier to do flat, even and

opaque areas with acrylic paint (I am still referring to large areas) while obtaining good gradations and washes with ArtistColors, because they are consistently transparent.

Oil pastels and ArtistColors

With this mixed-media technique we enter an entirely different field – these colours use different binders and, as a result, the oil pastels repel ArtistColors. You can create very interesting structures by working in a similar way to that just described for rough-surfaced paper. Using a suitable paper, apply oil pastels very lightly so that they adhere only to the raised areas of the paper surface. Now apply the ArtistColor; it will be repelled by the pastel. The result looks very different from the combination of ArtistColor and colour pencil because, owing to the more or less transparent nature of the media in these circumstances, the colours blend into each other.

This technique can be carried a step further by doing either a whole sketch or part of one in oil pastels, and then adding flat or gradated washes of ArtistColor. The example B of Illustration 16 (p. 44) gives you an idea of the effect.

It is possible to extend this technique further by using similar pastels with solvents or lacquer in conjunction with ArtistColor. This is discussed in the next chapter.

Conclusion

In contrast to a printed image, an original work of art always draws at least a part of its attraction from the materials with which it has been done. Because they might be able to convey exactly the effect you are looking for, the mixed media techniques described here are well worth investigating. On the other hand a 'pure' technique such as one of the watercolour methods previously described might suit you best. There is no way to find out which is the technique for you except by experimenting.

Very often in painting, the idea comes first, followed by the search for a way to realise it. But there are no rules for such matters. It is perfectly possible to discover or develop a technique first and then to start exploring the potential of the effect. But you should do something with any effect you master; in itself it is unlikely to sustain interest for long.

Pages 30 and 31 8. and 9. This picture of a cat in a tree is a typical example of the dry watercolour technique, while the rose in the barranco (dry river-bed in Spain) was done using the wet watercolour technique. Note the differences in structure and in colour impact. *Jutta Fischer-Brück*

29

Brocéliande

Jutta Fischer-Brück 1983

8
MIXED MEDIA II

Because they are composed of different binders and solvents, you cannot *mix* rotring ArtistColors with oils or lacquers. But by applying the principle described in the previous chapter, you can use them in combination to create interesting and unusual structures and textures.

There are two main ways to do this.

Separate application of media
You can, for example, apply lacquer to a sheet of watercolour paper and then, when it is completely dry, coat it with washes of ArtistColor. This will give effects resembling those obtained by combining oil pastels with ArtistColor as previously suggested. The problem here, however, is one of achieving an interesting pattern with the coat of lacquer first, because although it also tints the lacquer, the ArtistColor will emphasise the empty spaces between the lacquered areas.

A very common and interesting way to achieve intricate patterns is as follows. You fill a pan or large flat dish (which should be slightly larger than your sheet of paper) with water and drip a small amount of lacquer on to the surface (the kind used for cars or bicycles works best). As soon as the lacquer starts to form swirls and cloudy shapes you gently lower the paper on to the water and then remove it immediately. The lacquer patterns will transfer to the paper surface and it only remains to add washes of ArtistColor.

Simultaneous application of media
There is another and, in my opinion, more interesting way to use two media in combination. This is to apply both media at the same time. Illustration 16, example A (p. 44) shows one result. It was created as follows. The watercolour paper was first thoroughly soaked in water and then pinned to a board in order to prevent it from buckling. A weak solution of ArtistColor (about 20 parts of water to one part of paint) was then slopped on to the paper so that the layer of paint covered it thoroughly. Lacquer from a pressurised aerosol can was then sprayed on to the water and paint solution. It is important for the paper to be completely covered with this solution so that the lacquer cannot reach the paper directly.

These techniques can be varied and extended in many ways, but (as I have already suggested) you should not expect them to yield complete works of art. They will not, but they can form parts of pictures or backgrounds upon which you can then work.

Right 10. The intense brilliance of the colour was achieved by placing many layers on top of one another. The contrasting colours are bound together by a final coat of yellow. *Axel Brück*

9
BASIC COLOUR MATCHING AND MIXING

Up to this point we have been concerned with the technical fundamentals of painting or drawing with rotring ArtistColors. Now we will take a closer look at colour matching and mixing — a part of the process of handling colour which many beginners find daunting although it is really very simple.

The basic colours
For convenience, all colours except white, black and brown are usually arranged in what is known as a colour circle. It starts at the top with yellow, and then the cold colours (green, blue) form one half of the circle — down one side — and the warm colours (orange, red) form the other. These two half circles meet at the bottom with the colour violet. (Violet can be produced by mixing red and blue.)

It is possible to refine the colour circle and create intermediate values by mixing adjacent colours. This is what has been done in Illustration 4 (p. 22), which contains the original ArtistColors and intermediate hues in the sequence of the colour circle.

Familiarity with the arrangement of the colours in the colour circle facilitates easy matching and mixing — for example, colours that appear opposite each other in the colour circle mix to grey, while adjacent colours when mixed give intermediate values (see next chapter).

If you now add black or white you can, in turn, darken colours or lighten them. By mixing with brown you can also introduce a scale of the so-called 'earth' colours.

This straightforward arrangement for colour selection and control explains why it is best to work with a small but well-defined palette. Confronted with a large number of colours and possible combinations, you may not know where to begin. The small but well-ordered group of rotring ArtistColors allows you to keep an overall view of what is what and what does what.

This potential is further enhanced by the two mixing charts available, which I will describe after we have discussed the practical aspects of colour mixing.

Colour mixing
All rotring ArtistColors come in bottles with a built-in dropper. Simply by counting the number of drops, you can measure, very accurately, the amount of colour used. You can either mix the colours in your palette each time you use them or you can store the mixtures in small bottles.

There is no need to mix and store large quantities of mixtures, because you can of course achieve exactly the same colour again, provided you have made a note of the basic colours and the number of drops used.

You should never, of course, touch a mixed paint with a dropper, nor insert a brush (or nib) which has held a mixed colour, in the bottles which contain unmixed paints. Either will result in the contamination of the basic colour which will then make further mixing inaccurate.

With ArtistColor there is no need to mix large quantities of paint when you need only a very small amount of one colour in order to alter another slightly. Remember that just three or four drops of ArtistColor will carry you a long way and mixing, say, one drop of one colour with 60 drops of another could be very wasteful. If, instead, you were to dilute your one drop of the first colour with ten drops of water, and then use one drop of this mixture with six drops of the main colour, you would arrive at the same result.

This principle can be applied to all mixtures. Two examples are given below:

Aim:
Colour 1: 1 drop
Colour 2: 20 drops
Equal to:
Colour 1: 1 drop + 20 drops water
Colour 2: 1 drop
Use 1 drop of each

Aim:
Colour 1: 1 drop
Colour 2: 50 drops
Equal to:
Colour 1: 1 drop + 50 drops water
Colour 2: 1 drop
Use 1 drop of each

If you intend to store these solutions for a long time, just to be on the safe side you should use distilled water. (This applies to all water-soluble paints and is necessitated by the impurity of today's 'drinking' water.) Mixtures which you use up immediately will probably show no ill effects from dilution with normal tap water, although this may depend on the quality of your local water.

The mixing charts
With this book comes a two-part mixing chart (also available separately) which will serve as a guide for your first efforts in colour mixing. But please note that although much care has been taken in producing it, it has also passed through a printing process, which might affect its accuracy. Therefore the mixtures of the original paints may differ slightly from what you see in the printed chart.

On one side of the chart you will find mixtures of all the basic colours and also some intermediate hues. Each colour is mixed with each other colour twice: once with two parts of one colour and one part of the second, and then again the other way round. This results in 144 different colours, which you can either mix as they are printed or use as starting points for further mixtures. (For testing purposes we once produced 1500 different, systematically arranged mixtures in one go!)

If you now consider that you can produce, in addition, mixtures of three or more colours, you can imagine that there is no practical limit to what can be achieved by mixing the basic ArtistColor set.

A second chart, printed on the reverse side, has the same starting point — basic colours and intermediate hues — but this time shows the lightening of colours with white and their darkening with black.

Because some colours have greater covering ability than others, surprisingly different amounts of white (or black) are needed to achieve more or less the same degree of lightening or darkening.

The number of drops needed for each colour is given in the chart. You will see from this that, for example, you may need large quantities of one colour but only a small amount of the second to mix with it. This is where the suggestions given in the preceding paragraphs should come in useful.

Above 11. Placing a few drops of paint on a thoroughly wet watercolour paper results in this type of structure. This can be used as a background for a wide range of subjects.

Right 12. The juxtaposition of cold and warm colours can be used to create impressions of space and depth. Cold colours seem to recede into the distance, warm colours come forward. *Axel Brück*

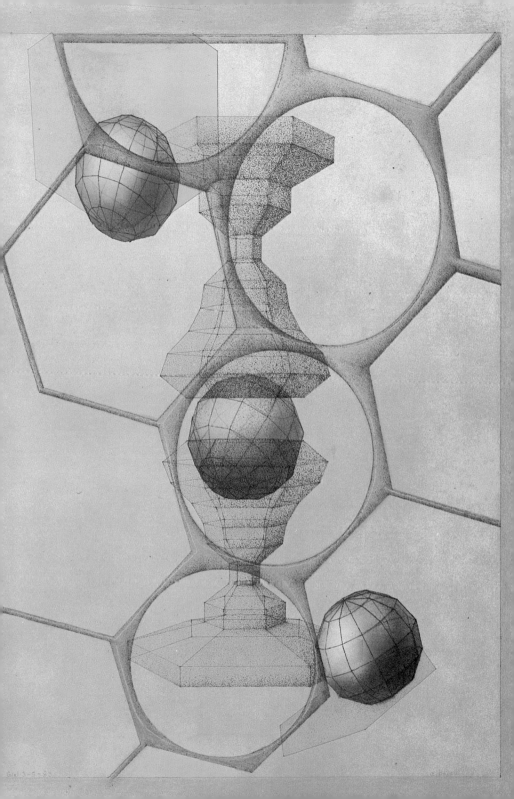

10
COLOUR MATCHING AND MIXING

We now move into a slightly more complicated realm — that of colour matching.

Colour matching

If you want to match a given colour (or if you have forgotten to make a note of the constituents of one of your own mixtures), you will need to deal with certain problems that do not arise in colour mixing.

First, you must take into account the fact that the *saturation* of a colour can differ according to the thickness of the layer. The relatively thick pool of paint in your palette always looks darker and more saturated than the thin layer on the paper, or other support.

Secondly, water-soluble paint tends to look darker when wet than when dry. This means that at first you can only mix an approximate colour. For the fine adjustments you have to test the colour out with the brush (airbrush, or whatever you are using), waiting until your mixture is dry before comparing it with the colour you are trying to match.

A third problem imposes another restriction. With transparent colours, a support which is even slightly off-white, such as the normally yellowish or greyish watercolour papers, tends to alter the overall colour of the picture. In such cases you must make your tests on the same support as the original. For these reasons *absolutely* accurate colour matching can be very bothersome and it is fortunate that you do not have to do it with your own work — assuming that you always remember to make a note of how you arrive at your mixtures.

'Optical' mixing

Up to now, we have only discussed the 'direct' mixing process, which is simply the creation of a new colour by combining one paint with another to produce a new one. There is, however, a quite separate possibility which, for many applications, yields superior results. Take an example: make green paint by physically mixing blue and yellow. But you can also make green by alternatively applying layers of blue and yellow to the paper (each layer should be thoroughly dry before you apply the next), so that no physical mixing occurs. This 'optical' mixing of colours (which works only with physically transparent colours like ArtistColors) is usually judged to be superior, because the resulting effect gives you a deep and vibrant colour that almost seems to glow. This effect is due to the reflection and absorption of light in the different layers.

Although working with multiple 'glazes' requires much more effort, I always feel that it is worth trying because the results really are superior.

If you look at Illustration 5 (p. 23) you will immediately notice the background which, in the original artwork, is almost pearly or opalescent. This has been achieved by using extremely thin layers of paint (I did not count them, but there were certainly more than thirty) in five different colours, with a final coat of white. There is no way in which this shimmering, iridescent effect could be achieved by physically mixing colours.

Another interesting example is shown in

Illustration 7 (p. 27). At first glance, the background seems to consist of gradated greys. But on closer inspection you will notice a bluish glow in some areas, which plays an important part in creating the overall effect. This was done as follows. The background was first covered with a solid black. Then a substantial layer of blue was applied. At this stage, because of the transparency of the paint, the background still looked black. Finally, a gradated layer of white was sprayed over the entire area. This brought out the very faint, cloudy bluish effect. (Unfortunately, the effect is greatly coarsened in reproduction, because such subtle differences are usually lost in the printing process.)

If you want to achieve effects of this kind you will always need to use optical colour mixing. But in other cases there is more flexibility. In drawings such as Illustration 1 (p. 18) there would be no point in using anything but pre-mixed colours because optical mixtures could not even occur. In most other cases you have the choice between optical and physical colour mixing.

Although I claimed earlier that optical mixing yields better results, I should say that this is a purely personal preference. Your purposes might be better served by the flat effects (no judgement intended!) obtained by mixing the colours physically. As always in art, there are no hard and fast rules.

Opaque colours

I have occasionally mentioned that ArtistColors are *consistently* transparent. This represents a considerable advantage over such paints as oils and acrylics, where some colours are transparent and others opaque. However, there are occasions when you really need an opaque colour. This can be achieved by applying a great number of layers or glazes on top of each other which, sooner or later, results in an opaque coat. But the simplest solution is to add a little white to the ArtistColor. A surprisingly small amount is necessary to turn the colour opaque. If you use only a very little and apply the colour in two or three layers, the colour change, compared with the original hue without white, will be practically indiscernible.

Page 40 13. ArtistColors can be made opaque by adding small amounts of white. This portrait has been executed on a flat wash. Note the effect of the partly transparent and partly opaque colour.
Jutta Fischer-Brück

Page 41 14. This nude was drawn with isographs, using only dots of similar diameter. This creates an entirely different colour-character from, for example, that seen in the illustration opposite, showing the versatility of the paint.
Jutta Fischer-Brück

40

11
PRELIMINARY WORK: THE SKETCH

After all these very important preliminaries we can now turn to how you set about making a painting or drawing. But *please note* that whole volumes can be (and have been) written about the topics that follow. Here, I can only indicate a few basic, and mainly technical, procedures. This is especially the case with my discussion about realistic representation, a subject that has, quite properly, received very detailed treatment elsewhere.

Preliminary sketches

To really master the wet watercolour technique you need to be able to solve all the problems of representation and composition in your head as you go along. But for as long as you lack the confidence to do this, you will need to prepare preliminary sketches. Let us look first at the method used to produce a sketch when a 'free' spontaneous approach is wanted. Here you make your sketches on ordinary paper, using a lead pencil and starting each new sketch on a clean sheet of paper. This should ensure that your design can 'freewheel' and stay fresh, even though you may be 'tightening' it constantly.

The significance of this is, perhaps, made clear when you look at the alternative method. Here you make your sketches on layout paper (which is semi-transparent) or on tracing paper. Both of these allow you to start a new sketch by simply placing another sheet of paper over the work you have already done and re-drawing the lines that you wish to retain.

This second method is the easiest for a beginner, but you should not use it without considering the long-term consequences. Working in this way tends to lead to highly formalised (some people would say rigid) compositions and strictly defined forms. If you are intending always to use the same method, then the choice you make between the two methods of producing sketches will, in time, influence your subsequent style enormously. If you have greater sympathy with the free and relaxed approach, you should adopt the wet watercolour technique, even if you find it more difficult.

Notable exceptions to this general statement are sketches for airbrush work. There you need well-defined and precise outlines in order to be able to cut masks. In this case working with tracing paper and refining the outlines is an essential part of the technique.

However, whatever the method, unless you feel able to make a complete sketch at the first attempt and then leave it as it stands, you should never work directly on to the watercolour paper. Subsequent corrections done with an eraser will damage the paper and the paint layer, resulting in ugly blotches.

Erasers

Quite apart from technical considerations, opinions vary widely on the use of erasers. Some experts suggest that they should never be resorted to because their use hampers the development of the artist's technical skill. Although I do not believe that the matter is as clear-cut as this, there is undoubtedly something in the argument. Rubbing out a line, putting it in again, changing it and rubbing it out again, over and over, will lead to confusion. It is actually better to finish a sketch at the first attempt and then start a completely new one to introduce improvements. If nothing else, this allows you to compare the various stages of your work and to make decisions based on your conclusions. This is preferable to having evidence of only the final stage and no scope for going back to the solution found at an earlier stage.

Nevertheless, one should not be dogmatic on this question and you should inform yourself about erasers. There are many types available but most are unsuitable for this kind of work. You need a very soft eraser for pencil and, if you work with ink on tracing paper, a special one for that too. (The yellow end of a rotring eraser is designed for ink and the white end for pencil.)

Kneaded rubber (also known as 'putty rubber') comes in handy for very detailed erasure and for use on delicate surfaces.

Transferring the sketch

Let us suppose that you have finished your sketch and want to transfer it to the support. If you feel sufficiently confident you can, of course, prop it up in front of you and then transfer it freehand to the watercolour paper. But the prospect of doing this is a bit daunting, even to an experienced person.

If you have done the sketch on tracing paper or on a semi-transparent layout sheet, there is an easier way. Turn the sheet over and trace the design with an extremely soft lead pencil (e.g. 4B) or with charcoal. Now turn it over again and place it carefully on your watercolour paper. Weight it down with a heavy object or hold it down with your hand and re-draw the design with a very hard pencil or a ballpoint pen.

This will produce a faint 'carbon-copy' of the sketch on the support. You can then either leave it as it is or work round the outline again with a pencil to reinforce the lines.

If you intend to use only very faint washes of ArtistColor the loosely adhering particles of lead or charcoal may pose a problem, because they can 'dirty' your colours. This may be prevented by retracing with a pencil and then carefully *rolling* (not rubbing!) the whole surface of the paper with a kneaded rubber − as stated above, a normal eraser would damage the surface − to remove the lead or charcoal orginally transferred. If your sketch paper is opaque, you will have to use the same technique as that employed for reducing and enlarging (see next chapter).

Page 44 15. (top) These two examples show different representations of the monotype technique, a printing method that results in 'one off' prints. For full explanation, see text.

Page 44 16. (bottom) The use of lacquer or other kinds of paint that cannot be mixed with ArtistColor produces some very interesting structures. Example A (left) lacquer and ArtistColor; Example B (right) wax crayons and ArtistColor.

Page 45 17 This is another example of the combined effect of opaque and transparent ArtistColor. Note that the colours have been used transparent and opaque (with small additions of white) to create the desired effect. *Axel Brück*

43

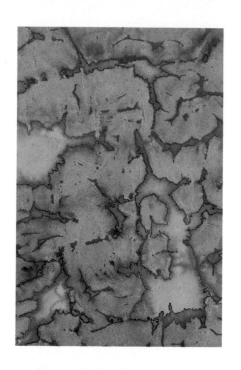

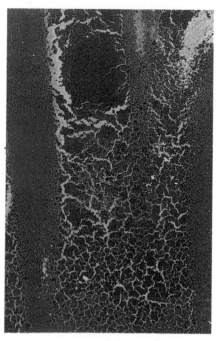

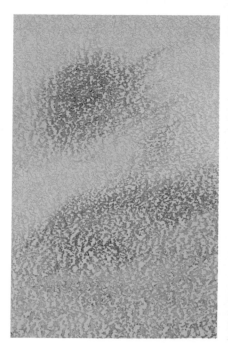

12
SKETCHES AND COLOUR
IN REALISTIC
REPRESENTATION

If you have made a sketch that is larger or smaller than the intended size of the finished work or if you want to work from a different source, such as a reproduction or photograph, or again, if your sketch is on opaque paper, then you have to use a special technique in transferring your sketch.

Reducing and enlarging

First, draw a grid on the sketch. This is usually done in 1cm squares. Then draw a similar grid on the support to be used for the final picture. Remember that you have to treat watercolour paper carefully, so draw only very faint lines with a soft pencil so that you can remove them with a kneaded rubber, as previously described. The squares on this grid must be larger or smaller, in proportion to the difference in scale between the sketch and the finished version.

If the shorter side of a sketch is, say, 30cm and that of the finished work 45cm, you would need grids measuring 1.5cm for the finished work.

It is now quite easy to reproduce the lines of the sketch, square by square, on to the support. The transferred drawing should be made with a harder pencil than the grid, so that it remains visible when you try to 'roll off' the grid.

Once you have successfully transferred the sketch, you can get down to the real work.

Using colours

Naturally, you should use your colours in a way that seems right to you rather than concerning yourself with colour theories or systems. Occasionally, however, things may go wrong. It is then quite useful to know something about colour. I can give only a few examples here. You can find out more either by studying nature (which can tell you most things about colour even if you do abstract work) or by referring to texts on the subject. This latter is the speedier process.

Garish colours in representational art

It quite often happens that the colours in a beginner's (realistic) picture look quite harsh or even garish, even though the individual colours are not particularly bright. Usually, this is because the various shades have been mixed without regard to the fact that colours in nature tend to influence each other — the blue of the sky is reflected in the shadows, a green meadow would throw a slight cast on to the wall of a nearby house, and so on.

An experienced painter will suggest these effects in his picture by adding traces of the surrounding colours to the one being mixed. These alterations in colour may be so small that a person looking at the picture does not even notice them. Nevertheless, they will draw the colours of a picture together, and thus avoid giving a garish or disjunctive impression.

To reiterate: it is not necessary to mix in a grey or muddy brown in order to achieve this. A very slight 'dirtying' or contamination of a colour with an adjacent colour is quite sufficient.

A very extreme example of this technique is shown in Illustration 10 (p. 33). Strongly contrasting colours are used, yet the picture remains cohesive and the colours do not even really clash. This is because the whole work was done with pure colours, straight from the bottle, but it also received a final overall layer of yellow. This yellow may hardly be visible in some parts of the picture, such as the background, but it is quite sufficient to hold everything together and to create a unified impression.

One reason why naive paintings *look* naive is that the painters do not follow the practice just described. (Another reason is that they do not include shadows in the picture, or only include the main ones.)

An extension of this technique, which could suit some subjects, is to paint a picture predominantly in one colour, for example, brown. If just one detail or a small part of the picture is then painted an entirely different, pure colour, such as yellow or red, this could create an effect that almost glows.

It is certainly not easy to secure such results but you can learn how it is done by carefully studying still life studies painted by the old masters — and by practising.

Natural colours

The technique just described could take you a long way towards achieving a natural rendering of colours. But this is by no means all there is to it. Generally speaking, there are no pure colours in nature. They appear only in man-made objects and even there they are often subdued or 'broken' by reflections from other coloured objects or by layers of dust and so on.

Probably the easiest way for a beginner to attain this more or less unified appearance in a work depicting natural subject matter is first to build up appropriate underpainting.

Earlier, I described a technique for dry watercolour painting. You start with a very thin relatively weak layer and then gradually build up detail and colour with additional layers. Applying this here, for the first layer you might use only a few closely related colours. For example, greenish-brown hues would be appropriate for a woodland scene. You would cover the whole painting, including even the sky, although the first layer should be very weak indeed. Using this method, an impression of unity comes about almost by itself, although the original first layer of colour may seem to be lost under successive glazes.

Above 18. Here the ArtistColor was mixed with acrylic binder which gives the effect of relief. The special luminosity was made possible by painting on a ground of gold leaf and is due to the consistent transparency of the colours.
Paul Sudheimer

13

COLOUR IN REALISTIC AND ABSTRACT REPRESENTATION

When we used the phrase 'realistic representation' earlier, it was in a rather loose sense. Looking at works of art of the last 150 years or so, it soon becomes apparent that there are many possible interpretations of the notion of realism. However, for the present purpose, it is sufficient to say that anything that allows you to recognise the subject which provided the inspiration for the work, is a realistic representation.

The degree of realism is obviously of some importance in this context because your handling of colour depends on it. Only with the 'photographically' exact approach is direct imitation of natural colours obligatory. In all other instances the choice is yours and, generally speaking, the freer your treatment of the subject the greater is your freedom with colour, too. The inference to be drawn from this is that in the wide and varied field of 'abstract' painting and drawing your freedom in handling colours is unlimited — or is it?

Colour and abstract work

Without making any attempt at a definition, one can probably say without fear of contradiction that an abstract work does not have a subject which is drawn in a recognisable way from the everyday world around us.

With realistic representation, the starting point is the natural colour of the subject. Deviations from this involve such matters as perception, association, viewing habits, etc.

In an abstract work it is quite different:

although the artist may have derived his idea from nature or a natural phenomenon, his subject is the colour itself. This gives rise to such questions as: what actually *is* a colour? How does it react with another colour? What are the relationships between different hues? How does the presence of one colour influence the perception of another? And so on.

Questions like these embrace an important class of subjects for abstract art and it would be natural for someone interested in colour (and paint as a material) to delve into this field with some enthusiasm.

But, curiously enough, many (adult) beginners are very reluctant to enter the field of abstract art. The reason for this is simply that they have failed to identify the challenge presented by its subject-matter — one subject being colour.

If someone were to approach a painting saying: "That is a marvellously painted rose, but this or that doesn't look very real", he would not be commenting on the artistic quality of the work so much as what he believes to be the technical skill of the artist. The comment may be based on the misconception that pictures should always aim to be as 'real' as possible, and the person making this comment may not have considered the fact that a deviation from nature may be quite intentional, because it can be used to express something specific.

This teaches us something about our subject: an abstract work is about something, even though this something is not a tangible object. The subject may be the problem of colour. Many artists have dealt with it in their work and their writings. There are also many non-artists who have created so-called colour 'systems' (such as the Oswald or the Hickethier system).

There is no space here to explain these intricate and intriguing systems and, in any case, the artist more often chooses an empirical approach based on his own instincts.

Basic colour concepts

A distinction is often made between 'warm' and 'cold' colours. The warm ones are orange, red and related colours. Cold colours are blue, green and others related to them. Yellow can be either, depending whether it contains a green or orange tint. The same applies to shades of violet, which can either be bluish and therefore cold, or reddish and warm. (Curiously enough, this is the reverse of what happens if you heat an object. It first glows red in the lower temperature range and, finally, blue at higher temperatures.)

The question of whether a colour is cold or warm is not purely academic because people tend to react differently to warm colours from the way in which they react to cold ones. The average person is said to feel attracted to warm colours and repelled by cold colours.

These different reactions are probably of more importance to graphic designers: the artist is more concerned with other aspects of warm and cold colours. Cold colours, for example, appear to recede from the picture plane, while warm ones seem to come forward. This is due to the fact that we subconsciously associate blue with distance. Indeed, it is difficult to pull these concepts apart: we refer to blue hills, blue haze and so on. This phenomenon is just one example of a subject that could be of interest to the abstract artist; it still works even where there is no identifiable object being portrayed, and an artist can use it to create spatial organisation in an abstract work.

On the other hand you could, of course, deliberately reverse the placement of colours, thus creating unusual spatial effects. This obviously works only with more or less realistic

representation or with precisely defined geometric objects. In an abstract colour pattern warm colours will always appear in front and cold ones in the background because the colouring is the only clue that is given to the viewer!

Note, for example, the rock formation in Illustration 9 (p. 31). This is rendered in a warm yellow while the rose in the foreground is blue and cold. It is mainly reversal of the norm in the placement of colour that gives the rose the curious impression of being detached – 'floating' in the picture, as it were. Another example is Illustration 14 (p. 41) where the meadow in the foreground is green (cold) while the sky has been rendered in (warm) orange-brown hues.

Illustration 12 (p. 37) shows a more 'natural' distribution. The grid or net in the foreground and the balls have been painted in warm colours, while the forms seen in the background and the background itself are distinctly cold. This greatly enhances the impression of space in the picture. The same applies to Illustration 1 (p. 18) where the impression of space has been enhanced by the choice of colours. It might be a good exercise to look through the other illustrations in this book (and, of course, other work) concentrating on this aspect, in order to gain a better idea of its possible applications.

Complementary colours

Warm colours are more closely related to each other than to cold ones. In fact, the strongest possible contrast is obtained by combining colours which appear directly opposite each other in the colour circle (refer to Ill. 11, p. 36). These are known as *complementary* colours.

Complementary colours have some interesting properties. If you mix them the result obtained is a more or less neutral grey. Note, however, that because the number of ArtistColors in the colour circle is uneven, one colour appears opposite two, so you cannot do this experiment in one step. You first have to mix the two adjacent colours. This results in a hue corresponding, for mixing purposes, to the simple colour found directly opposite in the circle. These two can then be mixed together to produce a grey.

If, for example, you were to dot a plane with equal amounts of complementary colours (you would have to make very small dots — a .13mm isograph would work), this plane would appear grey from a distance but dissolve into two distinct, brilliant colours when seen close up. This is due to optical mixing. You can also try glazes of complementary colours, as described previously. The same phenomenon is responsible for the grey seams that sometimes seem to occur in paintings, dividing adjacent planes of complementary colours.

Another useful application can be derived from the fact that adjacent complementary colours enhance each other; a colour appears more brilliant and luminous when surrounded by shades of its complementary colour.

In the previous chapter I described a method for making one particular colour in a picture look more brilliant. I mentioned as an example a picture painted in predominantly brownish hues with just one detail in pure red, or a related colour. You could enhance this effect by using a complementary colour for the detail (brown is not included in the colour circle, but it is a warm colour and therefore blue or green would do nicely). You could strengthen the effect further still by changing the main colour in the picture. For example, you could select a shade somewhere between orange and red and choose the blue-green (turquoise) immediately opposite for the detail.

It is rewarding to experiment with these simple effects, say by using one colour together with adjacent shades and then with various shades of its complementary colour in order to find out what effect this has on the whole picture.

Although studying books on colour theory is undoubtedly profitable, there is really no substitute for the practical experience gained by actually trying it out and by looking at the work of other artists.

All the artists I know constantly improve the quality of their perception by studying nature and the work of their colleagues.

I firmly believe that this is a profitable undertaking even if you do not want to become so deeply involved in respect of your own work.

14
MORE
ON THE EFFECTS
OF COLOUR

So far we have only discussed colour as colour, not as the physical substance, paint. One might experiment with coloured light or other ways of producing colour, but one could not hope to catch the rich qualities of paint as an artistic medium. The way in which you handle your paint — how you apply it — determines the kind of effect you will achieve.

Opaque and transparent application

I have already mentioned that you can make ArtistColors opaque either by applying many layers on top of one another or by adding small amounts of white. The following examples demonstrate how much the impression created can vary according to the way this is done. Illustration 17(p. 45) was done mainly with brown-orange hues of varying degrees of transparency. First, the ground was laid with a few gradated washes which were almost completely opaque. On top of this came some 'clouds' and dots of pure white. This increases the impression of opacity even further. (Compare this with any of the other illustrations that use the paper itself as the white and you will immediately see the difference.) This was the groundwork.

The actual drawing was placed on top of all this firstly by 'tinting' the ground with layers of transparent colour and then by adding more (opaque) white. This effect is very different from what would have resulted from using transparent colours alone.

Another example is Illustration 13 (p. 40). Here, too, the ground was prepared with

washes of opaque colours, while the overlaying colours are partly opaque and partly transparent. Some of the shading was added with coloured pencils. A thick layer of paint containing white has a relatively rough surface — resembling extremely fine-grain emery paper — so that the powdery character of the pencil work stands out well. (These details are, however, lost in the reproduction, which is greatly reduced in size.)

Incidentally, it is very interesting to compare these effects with the drawings, which are done strictly with lines and dots (for example, Ill. 14, p. 41). In this drawing all the colours were applied in dots of equal diameter (using a 0.13mm rotring isograph). All the variations in intensity and brightness are due to the number of dots placed on the paper and, therefore, to the amount of white paper showing through.

All these ways to apply colour can, of course, be combined to create very complex effects. (See, for example, Illustrations 12 and 17.)

Intensity of colour

You will have noticed by now that the effect created by the colours varies with the way in which they are applied. Colours that have been made opaque with white look more solid and flat — they have body and substance. If the colours are made opaque, or nearly opaque, by placing many layers on top of one another, they nevertheless retain a luminous, almost bodyless character. You can see the difference by comparing the illustrations mentioned before (Ill. 13 and 17) with Illustration 10 (p. 33), where the background and part of the subject has been built up in the layers.

If, after finishing a painting, you were to decide that you would have liked a slightly different degree of transparency, there is still something you can do. If you apply varnish to the finished, and thoroughly dry, work, you will notice that this results in a marked increase in transparency. The reason for this is that the varnish seeps into the paint and alters its reflective properties. (It also changes the quality of the surface, but this cannot be helped.)

If you try this, you must be very careful: any errors or blemishes in the under layers of paint which have been successfully covered by additional coats, will become visible again!

The ground

The colour and the surface of the ground have a considerable influence on the effect of your work. So far, I have assumed that the ground is white, but that need not necessarily be so. An extreme example of an alternative is offered in Illustration 18 (p. 48) where the support has been covered with gold leaf. This kind of ground reflects much more light than even the whitest paper and brings a luminous quality to the colours which can be achieved no other way.

Other types of non-white ground can work well but I strongly advise against using coloured paper or board. For one thing, these colours are not usually fade resistant, so your work will not last very long. Also, the colours available more often than not look flat and unappealing. The best, and indeed in my opinion the only, way, to have coloured grounds is to prepare them yourself. With rotring ArtistColor this process is quite simple. You lay a flat wash, nothing more. Nor are the possible uses of grounds prepared with ArtistColors restricted in the way that, for example, watercolour grounds would be, because they dry waterproof.

Transparent grounds

If one works on transparent grounds such as glass or Perspex it is usually because one wants colours to remain transparent. Light is either allowed to pass directly through the glass or the back of the support is covered with a highly reflective material so that the light passes through the layers of colour twice.

Naturally, the colour effects of these techniques require special handling. For example, opaque colours are out of the question, because they will look more or less like 'black holes' in the painting. Optical colour mixing would be especially effective, but the application of the individual coats must be very even because the transillumination (light passing through the transparent support) will emphasise even tiny differences in density.

Luminosity in pictures done in this way is even greater than that achieved with gold leaf and other metallic backgrounds. Unfortunately, transparent works of art are difficult to present (obviously, you cannot hang them on the wall) and impossible to reproduce in printed form.

When painting on gold leaf, metal or glass grounds, it is extremely important to clean the surface carefully, for example with nail-polish remover, window cleaner or ox-gall. The slightest trace of grease, even a fingerprint, prevents the paint from adhering properly.

Impasto painting

I mentioned earlier that ArtistColor can be thickened with acrylic binder so that you can apply it in thick, impasto (relief-like) coats. You may have wondered what purpose this would serve and whether it would not be better to use acrylic paint instead. The last illustration (Ill. 18) should answer these questions. We have already discussed the luminous quality created by painting on a ground of gold leaf. But more important is the special way in which the colours were applied. They were thickened with a considerable amount of acrylic binder which you can buy as acrylic polymer emulsion or polymer medium at artists' suppliers, and were then applied in a net or gridlike texture with a very fine palette knife. Apart from producing an even more luminous and translucent effect, the impasto application gives the paint a very irregular (almost facetted) surface which reflects and breaks up the light — thus adding a richness to the colour which could not be achieved in any other way.

This answers the second part of the above question. You could easily produce the same kind of texture with pure acrylic colours, but some of them are opaque, some semi-transparent and, again, some transparent, although none of them is as transparent as ArtistColor. Experiments have shown that it is extremely difficult to achieve similar effects by mixing acrylic paint with binder.

Although the example shown here is an abstract, you can, of course, use the impasto application of colour for all kinds of subject. Opaque impasto may have its uses, too.

Conclusion

When looking at the twelve small bottles, it is hard to believe that their creative potential is so great — it is a question of applying skill to bring them alive. I hope that I have been able to help a little by giving you some idea of the qualities of these paints.

Although I have been messing around with different paints for many years I still find it fascinating to experiment with colour, exploring what it can do and what one can do with it. I firmly believe that this is the right spirit in which to approach the matter — experiment, play around, gain experience, and then do something with what you have learned.

You may well ask, do what? But you will, in fact, probably find that you have some idea of what you want to do, if you have been interested enough to read this far, and if not, ideas are certain to develop as you get more involved.

With this, we conclude our short look at the uses and effects of colour and turn to some other aspects of painting which I have not yet touched on.

15
CREATING PATTERNS AND SHAPES

Having covered considerable ground as far as the 'how to' of using liquid colours is concerned, it is time to investigate the 'what' — the subject matter of your work. I have already explained that it is not only representational art that has a subject. Abstract art has subjects, too, but of an altogether different kind. It is perfectly reasonable to speak of, for example, geometric designs or patterns as subjects.

Most people find abstract subjects simple, compared with realistic representation, because they feel that they can do anything they want and whatever it is cannot be wrong. To draw, say, a few interlocking circles and then colour them in some way or other, does not pose any problems and is, indeed, a 'subject' hardly worthy of mention.

This, however, is not what I had in mind. Just as colour problems themselves become 'subject matter' when investigated seriously, so do geometric patterns and shapes. Five of the illustrations shown here should be proof of this: illustrations 5 (p. 23), 7 (p. 27), 10 (p. 33), 12 (p. 37) and 17 (p. 45) show nothing but very simple geometric shapes. But I prefer to believe, having done them myself, that these are, in fact, fascinating subjects.

It is usually not the geometric shape itself which is interesting, although some are intricate or intriguing enough to stand on their own, but its relationship to other shapes and its placement in the pictorial space.

This applies not only to three-dimensional shapes as they are presented here, but also to flat, two-dimensional patterns. With these, the pictorial space is not created by perspective but by the colouring alone, as previously explained.

From school or from your own experiments you may be familiar with the type of intricate pattern created by sticking pins into a board and then connecting them up with thread. Normally, this kind of work results in something that has merely a pleasing decorative effect. However, the various examples shown here perhaps suggest that this could also become a subject for 'serious' art by creating a unified effect, an ambience which gives it some meaning or a context.

You will have noticed the inverted commas around the word serious. I am not discussing Art, with a capital 'A', versus ornament and decoration, here. Suffice it to say that there is supposed to be a difference and that you are supposed to feel it, if you have the kind of sensitivity which makes you susceptible to the special merits of art. So I will restrain myself here and confine my advice to the purely technical matters of how to make ornamental and geometric drawings and paintings.

Compass and rulers
Realistic representations are nearly always done freehand, even with architectural subjects. In contrast to this, for geometric drawing you need drawing aids. First and foremost is the simple ruler with markings in centimetres or inches and the compass. Both

should be precision instruments and suitable for use with isograph pens. If you do this type of drawing quite often, a small drawing board such as the one shown on page 64 would be very useful.

It is a good practice first to make a drawing in lead pencil and then, if you do not want the outline of the shapes to be visible, leave it like that. Or you can subsequently re-draw it in ink. Remember that ArtistColor can be used in isograph pens, so that you can draw the outlines in any colour you wish, and you can even execute the whole picture with ArtistColor.

The type of compass that can be fitted with two points is very useful for transferring measurements when working on sketches or transferring them to the ground.

Templates and curves
Templates come in a wide variety of shapes and sizes. There are, for example, the elliptical or hexagonal variety, which can be very useful for geometric drawings. These have been devised for engineers and architects but this should not deter you from using them. Another group of shapes can be created with a set of french curves (Bezier curves) which you may be familiar with from your schooldays. All these instruments should have edges designed for drawing with ink. If they do not, you can adapt them yourself by gluing small pieces of paper beneath the templates. This will raise the surface sufficiently to prevent the ink (or ArtistColor from creeping under it and smudging your drawing.

Geometric drawing
The handling of these instruments is self-evident and needs no explanation. Arriving at a really satisfying figure or design for a fully-fledged work of art is a much greater problem. I think there are basically two ways that lead into it. Here is the first. Begin with the fact that all 'natural' subjects can be broken down into, or reduced to, simple geometric shapes or objects. (In some 'how to' books on painting and drawing you are taught realistic representation by starting with an ellipse for a face, and so on.) This could lead to compositions consisting entirely of geometric shapes which, nevertheless, look like

something and, to the viewer, provoke some associations with natural objects.

For example, the illustrations cited earlier in this chapter invariably remind people of landscapes or interiors. This is due to the arrangement of the objects and the peculiarities of the perspective, and not because the objects themselves resemble anything in particular — which they do not. This approach can be adopted with varying degrees of abstraction beginning, for example, with a cubistic rendering and then developing through different styles to the completely abstract type of work shown here.

Again it is quite interesting and helpful to study the work of contemporary artists (beginning more or less with the first years of this century) in order to find out what can be done and what has already been done by others.

Patterns and shapes
The second way to handle geometric forms could be called the 'pure abstract' approach. The above remarks apply mainly to three-dimensional geometrical objects. But similar things can be said about two-dimensional renderings — the true realm of patterns and shapes. In fact, any pictorial rendering, including the directly representational kind, can be described in terms of patterns and shapes. At present, however, I am referring exclusively to the 'abstract' variety.

Although many artists have used patterns and shapes in many different styles in their work, it was the once fashionable op-art that was entirely dedicated to this type of subject. If you are sufficiently interested, it can be very rewarding to study works in this style.

Op-art starts with such visual problems as the creation and development of optical illusions. These can tell you a lot about how our perception works. It goes on to the creation of spatial impressions with colours (which we have previously discussed) and shapes, and it ends up with very sophisticated effects of every kind which may excite your interest.

I will give you just one example. The triangular illustration (Ill. 18, p. 48) seems to consist of hexagonal shapes which partly merge or dissolve into the background, and of larger triangular structures with inconsistent outlines. You might imagine that this results from a conscious compositional effort by the artist — he might be trying to create a work simple enough to be bold and effective yet also ambiguous enough to invite curiosity and more detailed scrutiny. But this is not so.

This artist is interested in creating mathematically defined sequences of colours arranged in grids. Although these are precisely defined, it is impossible to say beforehand what the resulting picture will look like. In this example a sequence of ten colours was chosen, which begins at one point on the perimeter of the triangle and spirals inwards, the last colour always being followed by the first colour of the series.

There are many hundreds of possible permutations for each set of parameters which the artist has worked out — number of colours, sequences, inversions, starting point, number of elements in a grid, and so on. Each one leads to an entirely different 'composition', that is, to a set of structures and superstructures which the viewer finds visually appealing.

This example embodies just one set of subjects (or call it a set of visual 'problems' if you like) which do, indeed, merit careful investigation and yield fascinating works of art.

There are many other similar problems that might merit your attention. It is, for example, an interesting fact (and employed in some psychological tests) that viewers find some geometric or irregular shapes appealing, while others are more or less repellent. Some look pleasant, others more aggressive and still others quiet and restful. These various properties possessed by shapes can be enhanced by placing them in opposition to one another, by matching or repeating them or by using any other compositional means you can think of. Additionally, you can strengthen or weaken associations by colouring the shapes, or you can use colours to establish relationships or set up dissimilarities. You are the boss in this game and you can shape the worlds that you create according to your own intentions. But — and this is a big but — you can only get your world across to another person, someone looking at your pictures, if you really work at it. Playing around with nice looking patterns or shapes is certainly a pleasant recreational activity but it does not necessarily lead to the creation of works of art.

16
REALISTIC REPRESENTATION

We have already discussed some problems to do with colour and realistic representation, but the main question is probably still, how do you go about it? Unfortunately, this question is difficult to answer, despite the fact that realistic representation is not particularly hard to learn. In fact, anyone who has legible handwriting should be able to pick it up, given perseverance and will to practise. It is mainly a question of hand-to-eye coordination and of constant practice. This is exactly why it is difficult to explain in writing — there are no tricks or secrets to reveal, it is just a matter of whether you are willing to put in the effort to develop the skill. Nevertheless, I will make a few suggestions that might help the beginner to get started.

Observing nature
I have observed time and again people sitting with their sketch-pads to draw — let us say — a dog and, after some false starts and a lot of hesitation and rubbing out, giving up in despair, saying 'I simply can't draw a dog'.

This is the wrong way to start. The chances are that even an accomplished draughtsman could not do it this way. There are people who have specialised in a subject and who would be able to draw say, a dog, without referring to the live subject in front of them, but generally speaking every artist, even the most accomplished, needs to make constant reference to the subject he wants to draw, if the aim of the exercise is to produce a natural representation.

It is interesting to study naive paintings in this context. Although they are depicting 'natural' subjects such as people, trees, houses and so on, there is no attempt at realistic rendering. The naive artist draws or paints signs or symbols which represent the image of the subject in his imagination. So the question here is not really: 'How do I draw a dog?' but 'What does a dog really look like?' In other words, realistic representation is mainly a question of very close observation, of really *perceiving* what is around you. Normally, one tends to see a dog and think no more about it. But have you really perceived it? Did you notice its colouring or, for example, the proportion of its legs in relation to its body, or the length and shape of its ears, and so on? The likelihood is that you noticed none of these details, which means that you could never hope to draw it. This is why realistic representation is not concerned with just drawing a dog, but with drawing an *individual* dog.

Simple beginnings
If you now look at a dog very closely you will notice that it is really a very complicated subject and so not the ideal subject to start with.

In years gone by, the artist started his career in an academy by first learning to draw from plaster of Paris models of balls, cubes and pyramids, then switching later to bits and pieces of 'classical' sculpture. Much later this practice was frowned upon because it was thought to hamper the free development of the aspiring artist.

Carried to excess, these exercises would surely extinguish the creative fire in anyone. But the fact remains that trying to draw very simple things first — and sticking to them until you have mastered them completely — is the best way to learn realistic representation.

My advice is that you should start your exercises with an extremely simple still life. You could, for example, set up an apple and a vase (without flowers, initially) on a table or a piece of cloth and begin to study it. Do not rush into drawing right away. First look carefully at your subject and find out what it *really* is like. What is its shape? How do the parts relate to one another? Look at how the nearer parts hide the more distant. Does the subject have highlights and, if so, where? Where are the shadowed parts? Look at the shape of the shadows. And so on . . .

Only when you feel fairly clear about what the subject really looks like should you begin to draw it. But even then you should not attempt a fully-fledged painting straight away. Leave out the colour and start with a black and white drawing. Begin by defining the proportions of the subjects with a few lines or markings and do not go any further until you are satisfied with this first stage. This very important point applies to all stages of your work: if you go on to the next stage before you are fully satisfied with the preceding one, your drawing is bound to go wrong.

After you have set out the proportions, you might proceed by drawing the outlines. The next stage then would be to fill in the shadows and to define the highlights. This would leave you with something like a simple geometrical representation of the subject, which would then have to be brought to life by adding the texture and structure of the surfaces and, finally, some colour.

Another possibility would be to introduce texture and structure after the outlines and to fill in the shadows and highlights last. The sequence in which you work is actually relatively unimportant; the main point is to break down the work into manageable stages, which you can tackle and perfect one at a time. As you master the intricacies of each

stage, and your confidence increases, your style is likely to change and develop.

But at the beginning it is slow, step-by-step progress that carries you furthest. You should ignore those beginners who, with a few confident charcoal strokes, try to imitate what only an accomplished artist can do — to represent a subject with a few bold strokes that really do catch its essence.

As I have said, it is slow work. I advise the choice of a still life rather than a subject which is likely to move or change, or — like animals and people — to run out of patience.

The personal style

Sooner or later, anyone who keeps drawing and painting will develop a personal style. But the question of style should never arise in the early stages of learning (especially with representational art). The first, and most important, thing is for you to make a truthful and natural-looking representation of the subject. Later, you can introduce changes that reflect your personal attitude towards the subject. It should be obvious that you cannot deviate from your subject unless you first know how to represent it as it is. As long as you are dealing with realistic representations, the question of 'art' and 'creativity' is not relevant — either you can do a realistic representation or you can't. Other things come much later.

Structures and hyper-realism

The hyper-realistic or super-realistic style has been in vogue for some time now. It is very instructive to compare a painting termed hyper-realistic with a 'normal' realistic one. Or is there no difference?

In fact, there is a very great difference, and understanding what it is will help you in your own quest for realistic representation. Hyper- and super-realism are sometimes termed 'photographic' realism and this label identifies the main point nicely. A photograph shows the smallest detail, down to the threshold of visibility. A picture of a meadow, for instance, would show every single blade of grass (provided the photograph were large and sharp enough). The same applies to hyper-realism — the artist represents every detail in his painting with equal care and attention, irrespective of how important it is for the overall effect. Artists espousing this style usually work from photographs and determine the extent of detail shown in their painting by what can be discerned in the photograph(s).

A 'normal' representational painting would differ from this approach in this respect; if it shows a meadow, the fact of it being a meadow is the important point, not the distinguishing of the individual blades of grass. (This applies to a landscape painting. In a still life the threshold of detail could be different.)

So the representational (as opposed to the hyper-realistic) artist would not bother with thousands of blades of grass. Instead, he would employ what could be called a 'shorthand' — he depicts the overall impression of the meadow, i.e. its general structure, rather than every detail.

Another example: if you look at a piece of tree bark, you recognise the tree by the overall structure of this section and not by the tiny details. In a still life, you would paint the latter, in a landscape work with trees, the former.

The implication here seems to be that you should begin realistic representation with attention to the individual components of your subject and then, once you have mastered the initial stages, 'revert' to generalisation.

Such generalisation consists in finding exactly the right degree of 'shorthand' to suit your style and intention. It is impossible to lay down strict rules about how to represent a meadow, a wood, or tree bark, because all these things are an integral part of personal style.

Again, I cannot stress enough the value of studying other people's work. By seeing how different artists handle these questions you not only learn a great deal about their art, but also get some ideas about how to tackle a subject yourself.

17
PAINTING
AND DRAWING
FROM PHOTOGRAPHS

Some people strongly disapprove of the practice of drawing and painting from photographs, but this is not a very soundly based view. Artists have used photographs for almost as long as they have existed. It is certainly not a sign of a lesser talent if someone bases a drawing or a painting on a photographic source. Such figures as Picasso or Degas are sufficient proof of that.

It has already been mentioned that hyper-realists work from photographs. They have to, because it is a basic requirement of their style. But many other artists do it too because it is a very good solution to many practical problems.

However, drawing and painting from photographs is very different from working directly from nature. If you can do realistic work straight from nature you can just as easily work from photographs. But not the other way round. If you can work from photographs, this does not necessarily mean you will also be able to work from nature (although the dexterity acquired in this way will, of course, help).

Choosing a photograph
In taking the picture the photographer has already done part of the work, which would otherwise be done by the draughtsman or painter. The photograph is already an abstraction of nature — it is a composition. So you should think twice before you set out simply to copy someone else's photograph. It may already be a work of art in its own right.

If so, simply transferring it into a drawing or a painting is not only bad taste but ethically questionable, too.

On the other hand, it is perfectly acceptable to transform it, or use it only as a source of factual information about the subject. Your own photographs are an entirely different matter. Obviously, you can do with them whatever you want to and, if you take them specifically for the *purpose* of turning them into drawings or paintings, they will be the best kind of source material you can have.

Preliminary work
I have already described a way to transfer, reduce or enlarge a sketch with the help of a grid. The same approach can be used when making drawings from a photograph. You either draw the grid directly on to the photograph with a soft lead pencil, or you prepare a grid on a sheet of transparent plastic or cel and lay that over the photograph. If the photograph is your own and is in the form of a negative or a transparency, you can put it into an enlarger or a slide projector and project it directly on to the ground. The room should not be entirely dark — you need to be able to see what you are doing! Also, you must find a position for yourself that does not obstruct the projection of the picture. This takes a little getting used to but is about the only problem with this technique.

A third way to prepare the initial drawing is to use a pantograph. The pantograph is a simple inexpensive drawing instrument resembling lazy tongs, and is used for reducing or enlarging by tracing around the outlines of the subject. Some people like this instrument, others do not, but it must be said that it requires a certain amount of dexterity to use it and consequently it is mainly used for relatively simple subjects.

The artwork

It is, of course, possible to copy a photograph exactly. But you should first ask yourself whether this is what you really want. In my opinion duplicating the photographer's work is a vain pursuit. The photograph should serve as a starting point. You can, and should, for example, leave out unwanted detail — an option which the photographer does not have. You can also reinforce details which seem important to you. You can shift parts of the picture around and so change the composition. You can even assemble an entirely new picture by combining sections from different photographs.

This latter process, which could be called a 'painted collage' seems to me to be particularly interesting as you can do things that you could never hope to do when working directly from nature.

If you adopt painted collage as a technique, sooner or later you will produce some kind of surrealist imagery and a way of putting things together which is entirely your own.

A good way to set about it is first actually to make a collage. Cut out different images from photographs, prints, advertisements and suchlike and paste them together in a way that gives them some significance. After that, when you have become familiar with the process and its results, you can start drawing and painting them.

Realisation

The execution of the actual painting or drawing differs little from the processes already described. But it might be interesting to try out some additional techniques.

For instance, you could experiment with making a black and white painting from a black and white photograph. You could use mixtures of the ArtistColor neutral black and the white, in order to create the whole grey scale. Or you could use the wet watercolour technique previously described, but work only with the black in various dilutions.

An interesting variation on this technique would be to paint the major part of the picture in black and white but gradually turn into full colour for just one part of the subject.

For instance, a photograph may be blurred due to subject movement, or parts of it may be out of focus due to limited depth of field. Features such as these are rarely found in drawings or paintings. But it would be worthwhile exploring such pictorial properties in paintings and drawings and, indeed, some artists have done so.

The grainy structure of photographic enlargements belongs in the same category. Extreme enlargements of photographic negatives and slides display very peculiar structures both in black and white and in colour. These, too, could be worth exploring in paintings and drawings.

Another interesting aspect is perspective rendering. Whereas human perspective always remains the same, regardless of circumstance, a photographer can actually change the apparent perspective by using special lenses (such as fish-eye lenses) or he can change the perspective impression of the photograph, for example, by using extreme wide-angle lenses with certain viewpoints.

This 'visual vocabulary', which is actually the stock in trade of photography, can be used successfully in painting and drawing to create new effects.

If you begin working along these lines sooner or later you will discover a very curious phenomenon: many details that seem quite natural in a photograph simply look wrong when they are transposed to a painting or drawing. The viewer may feel that the angle of an arm or a leg is unnatural, even though they would never question the identical detail in a photograph. This is because we assume, without thinking, that a photograph *must* be right!

Conclusion

As you can see, there is nothing disreputable about working from photographs. It simplifies your approach to subjects, which otherwise might be beyond your reach or too difficult to handle. Moreover, photography itself offers interesting visual phenomena which can enrich the painter's vocabulary and can even lead to discovering entirely new subject areas.

Final remarks

This discussion of some aspects of drawing and painting has, of necessity, been very short and therefore, at least in parts, sketchy.

Nevertheless, I hope I have helped to set you on the path of exploring creative possibilities. The aim has not been to confront you with a profound theoretical discussion of art or a technical analysis of painting materials. Both these things, although interesting, would not help you in the initial stages of your journey. What you need is what some artists call a 'good eye' and an understanding of what can be done with the materials you use. To acquire both of these is mainly a matter of practice and, perhaps, a bit of advice in the right place at the right time. There is no substitute for actually *doing* things. If you do not get your fingers into the paint (or even your arms up to the elbow!) you cannot expect artistic achievements of any kind.

There are some people who believe that art (whatever that may be) is to be numbered among the superfluous things in life. Others know better. Once you get really involved in one way or another, that is, either by doing it yourself or as a spectator, you will realise soon enough that you can no longer live without it. Art is addictive and if my efforts have helped you to become hooked, this book will have served its purpose.

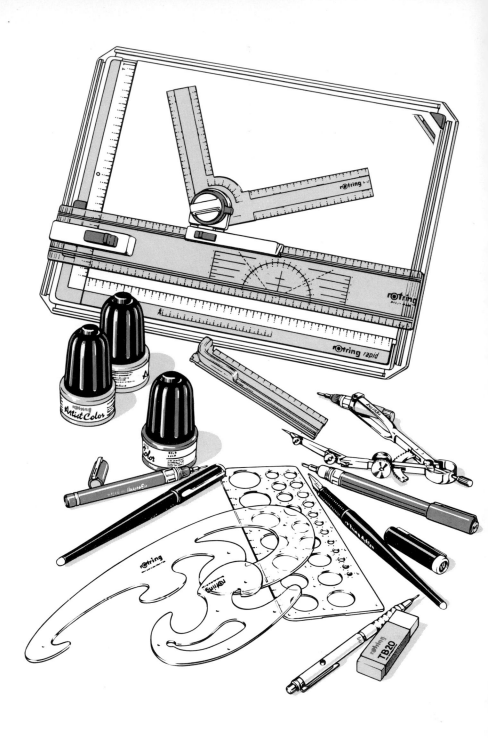